LET'S LOOK FOR TREES

HOW TO USE THIS BOOK

If you look outside, you will probably see at least one tree. These incredible plants provide food, medicine, furniture, homes for creatures and even the pages of books like this. Use this guide to...

...read about the magnificent world of trees and discover what is so amazing about them.

...take outside with you to see what trees you can find and identify, then tick off the ones you see.

...have fun playing with the tree stickers on the fold-out woodland play scene at the back.

What is a tree?

Trees are the largest plants on Earth and they often live for a very long time. Most trees have a woody stem with branches and leaves growing out from it.

Leaves and buds

Leaves are needed to make food from sun and air. Buds are new leaves or flowers waiting to unfurl.

Crown

This is the upper part of a tree that includes the leaves and branches.

Trunk

This transports water and minerals from the roots to the rest of the tree.

Branches and twigs

These take food and water to and from the leaves, flowers and fruits.

Roots

Roots absorb water and minerals from the soil and keep the tree fixed in the ground.

Amazing tree facts

Why is it unwise to eat too many apple pips?
What do you think is the tallest tree in the world?
Find out the answers and learn other facts below.

Leaves from the bay laurel tree were used to crown the victors in competitions in Ancient Greece.

The world's tallest trees are California redwoods, which can grow to be about 115 metres (379 feet) tall.

The tree line describes the point above which trees cannot grow because of freezing conditions.

Sticky buds on trees keep away insects that otherwise might eat them.

Trees use the carbon dioxide that we breathe out and change it into oxygen that we breathe in.

The word "book" comes from an old word for beech, as strips of beech bark were once used for writing on.

Apple pips contain a small amount of poison, so don't eat too many!

Medicine called aspirin comes from the bark of some willow trees.

Tree-spotters, turn the page!

Easy-to-spot trees

You are most likely to see flowers on trees in the spring, and fruits, nuts and seeds in the autumn.

Tick them off as you find them.

Harder-to-spot trees

aspen
laburnum
eucalyptus
magnolia
Douglas fir
spindle
pear
whitebeam
box
monkey puzzle
cedar

New beginnings

Trees come in many shapes and sizes and most of them start life as a single seed. This is the story of how an acorn turns into a large oak tree, providing homes for many other plants and animals.

FROM SEED TO TREE

1. An oak tree produces flowers in the spring.

2. Pollinated flowers turn into acorns with seeds inside them.

3. When an acorn falls to the ground, it may be buried by animals or by the wind.

4. Roots start to push down out of the seed, taking up water and food.

5. The stem sprouts upwards, and leaves begin to form.

6. A tree starts to form and carries on growing and growing.